Vultures Eat

Kristina Rupp

This is a vulture.

Vultures eat meat.

Vultures don't kill what they eat.

What they eat is dead before they find it.

Vultures like to eat animals that have been dead for a short time.

The animals they like to eat the most only ate plants.

Vultures eat dead meat that could make other animals sick.

But vultures don't get sick.

This vulture wants to eat.
How does she find her food?

She flies up high to look for food.

She can see very well.

She can smell very well, too.

She can see and smell dead animals from far away.

There's something to eat!

Is this a dead animal that she likes to eat?

Yes! It hasn't been dead very long and it ate plants.

She eats as much as she can.

Other vultures could come to take her food.

After her meal, she cleans her feathers. Feathers are hard to clean. If she isn't clean, she could get sick.

She doesn't have any feathers on her head. It helps her stay clean.

21

What she eats is gross,
but what she does is good.

Too many dead animals can make animals and people sick.

23

Vultures help keep the land clean.

Turkey Vultures

Turkey vultures have an amazing sense of smell. They are one of very few birds of prey that find food with their nose.

Their six-foot wingspan and light body (weighing no more than 5 pounds) let them glide in the air for hours without flapping.

When a turkey vulture is scared, it plays dead or throws up its last meal on its attacker.

Turkey vultures may look like hawks or eagles, but they are more closely related to storks.

North, Central, and South America are all considered home to the turkey vulture.

To stay cool on hot days, turkey vultures pee down their legs. This also helps kill harmful germs.

Tricky Words

before
very
after
find
people
only
much
away
other
long
something

Use words you know to read new words!

for	my	can	eat
fort	by	pan	meat
sort	why	pant	mean
short	fly	plant	clean

Word Attack Strategies

Stop	**Stop** if something doesn't look right, sound right, or make sense.
	Look at the **picture**.
s___	Say the **first letter** sound.
sh___	**Blend:** Say the first two letters.
⟵	**Reread:** Go back and try again.
▇ort	**Cover** part of the word.
sh(o)rt	**Chunk:** Look for parts you know.
sort fort	Think of a word that looks the same and **rhymes**.
blank ⟶	Say **"blank,"** read on and come back.
a e i o u	Try a **different sound** for the vowel.